This book belongs to:

....

First published in 2013 by Hodder Children's Books
This paperback edition published in 2014

Text copyright © Mij Kelly 2013
Illustrations copyright © Charles Fuge 2013

Hodder Children's Books, 338 Euston Road,
London, NW1 3BH
Hodder Children's Books Australia,
Level 17/207 Kent Street, Sydney, NSW 2000

A catalogue record of this book is available
from the British Library.

ISBN 978 0 340 98128 3

Printed in China

FSC
www.fsc.org

100%
Paper from well-
managed forests
FSC® C104740

Friendly Day

Mij Kelly and Charles Fuge

Hodder
Children's
Books

A division of Hachette Children's Books

When Cat caught Mouse, outside his house,
courageous Mouse cried, "Hey!
Put down that plate and see the date.
It's **Friendly Day** today

` a day for sharing, a day for caring,
when everyone is nice,

when Frog reads Snail a fairy tale
and cats do NOT eat mice."

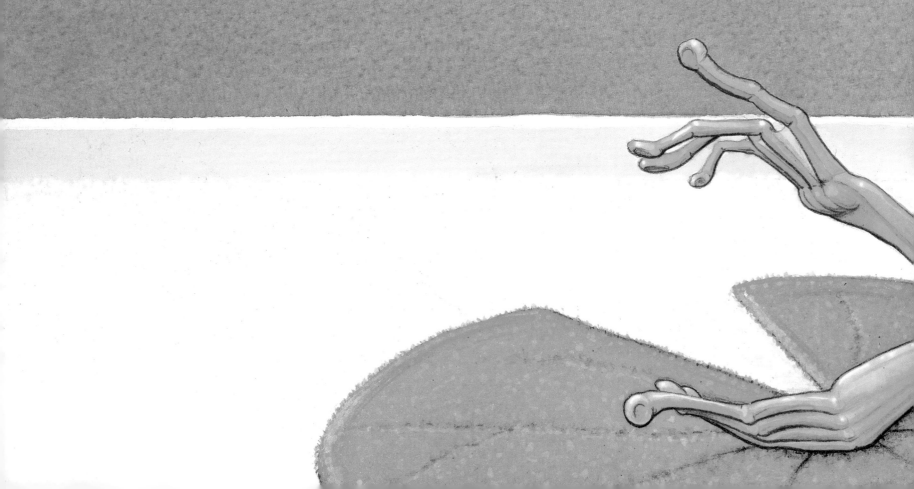

"Well fancy that," exclaimed the cat,
"I'll *have* to spread the word!"
He quickly strode across the road,
and told Dog what he'd heard.

Dog stared wide-eyed, and then replied,
"That's such a great idea!
You mean to say, today's the day,
the one day in the year

when parakeets bring tigers treats
and Rhino takes the time
to knit new mittens for helpless kittens
and sing a nursery rhyme?"

Cat cried, "Yes! Yes! And sharks play chess with all the little fishes,

and old grey Moose pours orange juice for anyone that wishes,

and even Mole comes out his hole
to play 'I Spy' with Goat

and Chimpanzee makes herbal tea
for Ostrich's sore throat."

Dog said, "Oh boy, what joy, what joy!"

And "Hip-hip-hip hooray!"

He called, "Hey Bear, are you aware,

today is friendly day

when foxes croon all afternoon
to entertain the geese,

and little birds tweet soothing words
of hope and love and peace."

Bear scratched his head, and then he said,
"It is a lovely thought,

to think that we could ever be,
as kindly as we ought.

To think baboons hand out balloons
to all the butterflies,
makes tears of bliss and happiness
come pouring from my eyes."

"But Dog," said Bear, "Are you aware,
there's really no such thing
as friendly day, or any day
when wasps and bees don't sting?

I must insist, it don't exist.
It is a lovely lie."
Poor Dog. Poor Cat. They hated that.
They both began to cry.

Inside his house, the tiny mouse
was glad he'd slipped away.
He'd tricked the cat, but now he sat
and longed for **friendly day.**

Meanwhile, outside, the dog still cried.
The bear gave him a pat.
"Oh, do cheer up, my dearest pup.
I have a plan," said Cat.

We'll talk to Snail and Snake and Whale.
We'll put the world to rights.
We'll make them see how things could be,

if only no-one fights."

Dog thought of how a friendly cow
might **help** a crocodile,

how centipedes might do
good deeds...
He smiled a watery smile.

Then **arm** in **arm**, with old-world charm
— and so much to be done —
the **three friends** strode off down the road,
towards the setting sun.

If you enjoyed this heartwarming tale, you'll love…

One More Sheep
Mij Kelly and Russell Ayto
"...works to perfection." THE TELEGRAPH
978 1 444 91030 8

Ellie Sandall
COPYCAT BEAR!
978 1 444 90158 0

The Bump
The story of your mum's love for you.
Mij Kelly & Nicholas Allan
978 0 340 98950 0

"Book a ticket for this fanciful ride to dreamland." Publisher's Weekly
WILLIAM and the NIGHT-TRAIN
Mij Kelly and Alison Jay
978 1 444 91029 2

Bears, Bears, Bears!
Martin Waddell
Illustrated by Lee Wildish
978 1 444 90679 0

NURSERY TIME
MIJ KELLY
MARY McQUILLAN
978 0 340 99926 4

For fun activities, further information and to order, visit www.hodderchildrens.co.uk